M000297528

WITCH
HUNT

POEMS BY JULIET ESCORIA

For Scott

Lazy Fascist Press
PO Box 10065
Portland, OR 97296

www.lazyfascistpress.com

ISBN: 978-1-62105-217-3

Copyright © 2016 by Juliet Escoria

Cover photo by Scott McClanahan

Cover design by Matthew Revert
www.matthewrevert.com

All rights reserved. No part of this book may be reproduced or transmitted in any form or by any means, electronic or mechanical, including photocopying, recording, or by any information storage and retrieval system, without the written consent of the publisher, except where permitted by law.

Printed in the USA.

CONTENTS

AXL ROSE AND OTHER MEN

HOW DO I MAKE THE BAD THOUGHTS STOP

BIPOLAR NATIONAL ANTHEM

NATURE POEMS ARE BORING

RELOCATION

TRUE ROMANCE

FEAR AND SELF-LOATHING IN VARIOUS STATES

ANXIETY ATTACKS

WITCH
HUNT

AXL ROSE AND OTHER MEN

WHATEVER USELESS THINGS

When he kissed
me there was only
one more thing
I wanted and that
was to completely
disappear.
The mornings left
my insides sore
and the outer part
of me in a dust
film broken
pieces of skin
and no dreams
remembered.
He did not regret
his wanting
although he
may have regretted
the fulfillment
but what else
is there
to say about
desire.
The answer is
disappointing.
The answer is
not much.

DAVID FOSTER WALLACE'S ROCK IDOL WAS AXL ROSE

In the music video for "November Rain,"
Axl marries and then kills off his
in-real-life girlfriend Stephanie Seymour.
I think you'd have to not much believe
in the power of your magic,
or whatever you want to call it,
to do something so stupid like that.

But maybe Axl was aware and just didn't care,
just wanted to see what he was fucking with.
Maybe he wanted Stephanie to be dead,
incapable of letting anyone but him
love her ever again.
Maybe he wanted her beautiful body
to rot away,
maybe he knew that we all look
the same
when we've been dead for long enough.

Anyway, she didn't die
so maybe Axl just isn't that good
at magic.
Instead of marriage or death,
they just assaulted and sued
each other a couple of times
which I guess is a
lesser kind of marriage,
a lesser kind of death.

EMOTIONAL TRUTH

Axl Rose is wearing
tight leggings patterned in roses
his penis popping large as a
tube sock
body shaking on the
sexy psychologist's recliner
in a way that seems too ridiculous
to ever happen in real life
except VH1's Behind the Music said
he was undergoing intensive therapy
at the time of that music video
so maybe that's the way to dress
if you want to heal.
Maybe I'm doing it
wrong.

LOSE MY DELUSION

His hair was a puddle
on fire wet for
slippage burning for
slickness and there was
a reason he married
only the once. Hips
don't lie, a wise man
once said, and his
were no
exception because
under his jeans I found
truth.

Angels drowned
beneath his skin it is
their light with which
he remembers it is
their light which allows
him to forget
Indiana because
if that didn't happen
then how could one
truly inhabit
those shorts besides
everyone knows
geniuses don't grow
in the Midwest,
just corn.

TODAY'S TAROT SPREAD

I do not know your fate but
I am certain it does not involve
loving me.
Just wanted to let you know.
Figured it might make you happy.
Maybe not now but
in the long run.

WILD WEST

"Cowboy Song"
is about a Black
Irishman
who wants to tame
some ponies
and I think I'm the kind of girl
who could let him

I'd take him on a quiet ride
down into the dirt
show him how there is a place
on the horizon where everything
bleeds the same same same

Oh but when it storms
the thunder claps
box your ears with
violence
it will witch you away
if you are not careful
it will make your
nose bleed

the thing they never told him
back on the other side of the world
is what happens when the cowboying
goes wrong

I remember a ranch house with two
cowboy sons
the younger did heroin and
it got real bad until

one day the older found him
dangling from the rafters
years later the voices spoke
and paranoia lifted him
he took a rifle and blew apart
his head
there were spiders in the walls
the sunsets blew out trails of bats
and everything was
just how he imagined

we drank from two glasses of
ice cold Coca-Cola
I made a promise about
transferring money into
his bank
but the truth is
there are only three things
you can do with a man like that:
forgive,
forget,
throw away.

ROMAN CANDLE

Listening to Elliott Smith
reminds me of the time
I was girlfriend to a junkie
and we lived in darkness
except for afternoon trips to a diner
where he nodded out over eggs
and I felt mortified each time
even though most meals
were interrupted by me
running to the bathroom
to vomit.

At some point we changed places
but I didn't notice until
I was on top of mailboxes
a block away from my apartment
because I had fallen asleep again
while driving.

29TH STREET, MANHATTAN

The best catcall I ever got
started out regular,
with the man saying,
Hey baby.

I had just left my therapist
where I started
crying uncontrollably
in the middle, and left
feeling shaky
and split open,

so I was in no mood.

He was with his friends
and changed his
tune so fast:
calling me stank ass,
and that no one wanted
me anyway,
that I needed
to eat some chicken
and eggs.

I think maybe he meant
steak.

I yelled at him
to fuck off, faggot—
a thing I would not
normally say but
it had the

desired effect.

I got onto the subway
before something
worse could happen.
I never went back
to that therapist.
She called me several times,
wondering if I was OK,
but it seemed impossible
to call back
or pick up the phone.

CASUAL MISANDRY

Maybe I would write about
Cocks
If they weren't so
Stupid
If they didn't
Resemble dumb
Noses waggling in the
Air
They're not like
Vaginas
Complicated
And interesting
They are just
Billy clubs
Mistaken by
Blind people
For guns.

Here is a joke I know:
Gentlemen,
Look in your
Trousers.

Here is another:
Q. How many
Cocks
Does it take
To change a
Lightbulb?

A. Zero
Because
They're
None
Too
Bright

JUST THE TIP

When
Writing
Poem
It
Best
To
Be
Hungry
Although
Not
Always
For
Food

LETTERS TO EX-LOVERS

DEAR PATRICK

I'm not sorry for forgetting your address or your phone number, but I must admit I do have some regrets about the loss of your face. When I think of you there is nothing anymore, just static.

So I don't remember what you looked like the day you took me down to the beach, how your voice sounded, what you said. I do remember there was no one around and your hands were hot and sticky. I remember how it seemed like something bad would happen later and it did. I never meant for it to escalate that way, I just wanted you to stop yelling. I was picking glass shards out of the carpeting of my car for weeks.

DEAR COLIN

I spent nearly every night with you for a month, but I don't think I ever learned what you cared about. Sometimes you claimed to have spent the day making music, not the real kind but by using a computer. Whenever I asked to hear, you said it wasn't ready.

The only food you ever ate was that prepared by other people. The only thing in your fridge was take-out leftovers, beer, and vegan ice cream. You claimed to care about health, hence the veganism, but I never saw you without a cigarette. You told me once you'd never been in love but spoke so fondly of an ex it was hard to believe you.

I decided to go away for the summer. When I came back the emptiness had gone which meant you'd outlived your purpose. I went over to your apartment anyway. You alluded to having had other relationships while I was gone, but your browser history showed too much porn for that, even for you. I never got the chance to hear you speak an honest word. I wonder if that's even something you know how to do.

DEAR JOHN

I tried to not judge your drinking but it was hard sometimes. I'd come over and the sun wouldn't even be down and you'd be slurring your words already. By the time I'd had a few, you'd be blacked out, belligerent, yelling about something or another for no reason.

You had so much anger toward your mother. I guess you didn't like the fact that she'd succumbed to cancer, and maybe because your brother hung himself shortly after. You blamed her death for his, which seemed really unfair. You only ever spoke of it when you were drunk so I never understood the logic, or if there was any.

I laughed at you when you ended it, not because of the end but because of your reason: I drank too much. But your next girlfriend was that sweet girl with the high-pitched voice and the love for Jesus. I guess you wanted someone to save you. I will be the first to admit— that was never one of my strengths.

DEAR MICHAEL

You brought us home after the bar closed and offered to make us some cocktails. The liquor was new, you said, expensive, had notes of berries or butter or something else that made it seem high class, and my friend was interested in that type of thing. I came along because I was feeling agreeable.

I remember falling limp, the embarrassment at the loss of control over my limbs. I woke up later in your bed, the blankets pulled over my body, my clothes folded neatly on the floor, my mouth tasting of vomit. My friend had disappeared, as had yours, and the apartment was silent. You were at the foot of the bed watching sports on mute. There were no lights on.

I don't know what happened in that bed while I was under. Maybe nothing. I would have asked but I didn't know you well enough to phrase it in a way that didn't sound ugly. I did not feel violated, then or the next day or even now. You never caused me pain. The only thing you gave me was a question: What happened during that time, in that space? And if you did something bad, and I never knew about it – does the bad thing have no weight? Does it not matter?

DEAR PHIL

I wore blue to court, a button-up shirt with ruffles down the front I had bought especially for the occasion. I heard somewhere that blue was the color of innocence. The public defender they assigned me was young and had greasy hair. She seemed sad. You were there, with your mother, so I guess that meant you two were talking again. I didn't want things like that to go well for you. I wanted for your mother to hate you, to see you the way that I saw you. I wanted for you to hate yourself. I wanted for you to die.

The restraining order passed, but I had no proof for the property damage and I had not photographed the bruises. They told me if you violated it, I should call the police, which left me unsure of the restraining order's purpose. But you left me alone from then on out, so I guess it worked.

Sometimes now, a decade later, I still look at your Facebook. For a long time it appeared like you didn't have a job and I hoped it was because I had ruined you, but it seems like you're doing better now. Your string of girlfriends has turned progressively less attractive, a fact I hold on to tightly, because I need some tangible evidence that I won, that you lost, that I beat you.

DEAR AARON

I did not want a relationship at the time, but then again I never do. You went to my party. I'd never seen you before but no one had anything bad to say about you, so I let you stay over and after a while you never really left. I would not let you fuck me. I had no good reason for this, I just didn't want to. I couldn't figure out why you stayed around, why you wanted to hold me, why you wanted to sleep in my bed, why I wanted you to. Sometimes the worst thing to be is alone.

One day I came home from work and you were smoking meth on my couch. I didn't get mad. Instead I joined you. We were up for several days. At the end, we had sex and it went poorly, so I locked you out of the apartment when you went for a cigarette. You mistook my neighbor's door for mine and banged on it for over an hour. The police were called. I never saw you again. I felt like I should care, about any of it, but I didn't have any thoughts on the matter either way. I heard you left town after that. Good riddance.

DEAR ROBBIE

At that point, you had figured out you were mostly gay but were still experimenting with women. You said you liked me because I was a pinup come to life, with my Bettie Page bangs and red lipstick. I was easily flattered so I said yes to dinner. We went through three large sakes before I took a trip to the restroom where I dry-swallowed a 5mg Oxy. By the time I said yes to going back to your apartment a thick fog had descended over my brain.

The first thing you did was blindfold me. From there you took off my clothes, bound my wrists and attached me to some set-up you had installed in your doorway. The objects you hit me with and the objects you inserted into my body made me feel like an object myself, something free of a voice and free of thoughts. I assumed that, as a man with an amateur dungeon and that many sex toys, when you inserted yourself you'd include a condom. Later I figured out this wasn't the case. By that point, I couldn't get mad because I hadn't asked.

When you were done with me, I went onto your patio, without speaking to you or dressing first, and smoked a cigarette. You lived on a hill; from your balcony I saw lights and then lights, a band of darkness and then, miles away, the constellation that made up Tijuana. I thought about the people who might be in that band of darkness so late at night, trying to cross undetected from one side to the other.

The air was cool and gave me goosebumps. I blew out smoke and everything inside me was empty and still, as though you'd beaten out the dust. A few weeks later I went to Planned Parenthood, where I was asked if I'd "engaged in any high-risk activity," and I didn't know what to say, not knowing the equations necessary to calculate the severity of risk.

DEAR MATTHEW

I was trying to get clean and I just couldn't figure out how to settle my mind. I'd forgotten a set of house keys at your apartment the week before while blacked-out, and it occurred to me that you might do the trick when I went to retrieve them. I was wrong. Being naked with you, dead sober, just made every thought ring louder, an inescapable roar coming from the failure of our limbs to find some sort of meaning in the hallway light. I left when you went to use the bathroom because I didn't know how to say goodbye.

The next time I saw you, something had gone wrong. You weren't making sense and didn't have a home and were missing at least three of your teeth. I know from experience that it's difficult to distinguish the consequences of mental illness from those of drugs, so I don't know if it was meth or crack or something less preventable, maybe schizophrenia. By then I'd completed another degree and had nine cavities filled. We are told that that kind of sickness isn't contagious, but I couldn't get it out of my head that I'd infected you. .

HOW DO I MAKE
THE BAD
THOUGHTS STOP

RECURRING INTRUSIVE THOUGHTS

Sometimes when I think about myself, I see my body on the beach. Except there is no water. So I guess it's actually a desert. I see my body in the desert, splayed across the sand and the sun is very bright. It is hot. It is so hot that my skin gets soft, a little softer, and then it begins to melt. My nose flops over first, and then my thighs go, and my breasts are dripping down in rivulets, across my ribcage, trickling down my armpits. My organs sludge out too, staining the sand wet, and then all that's left are my bones. I am very skinny.

Sometimes when I'm having a conversation with someone else and it's boring me or I don't like where it's headed, I think about grabbing the other person by the hair and bashing their face into the wall. It doesn't matter where the actual conversation is taking place; in my mind the wall is always made of stucco. It's cream-colored, the kind that is very common in the southwest. Their nose goes in first, and you can see the bone, the depths of their sinus cavities, and then their teeth chip away like lumber. The scalp separates and I am holding the bloody hair in between my fingers, wondering where it all went wrong.

Sometimes when I look at a cute baby or an animal I think about it getting run over by a train and the noise it would make.

Sometimes when I'm trying to fall asleep I think of a giant, ripping the roof from my house like a sardine can and plucking me off into the night. He takes me home and lays me out on a baking sheet and I am too scared to run away. I'm put in the oven and it is very warm in there and it makes me sleepy. I am left in there for a long time. It feels like decades. Eventually I am all dried up and crispy, so the giant takes me out and chops me into a fine powder and lines me into rails and then he snorts me.

Sometimes when I'm going to get crackers or cereal from the cupboard, I feel fear when I open the box and expect the container to be filled with maggots, with flies buzzing out. Sometimes I hold the box to my ear and shake it a little to make sure I don't hear any squirming inside.

Sometimes when I'm on airplanes I think about me dying, because someone put arsenic into my coffee or something. I stop breathing and my skin turns a little blue. My eyes bulge. I am slumped against the window, and there is blood pouring out my nose. It stains the seat.

Sometimes when a friend calls me on the phone and they want emotional support, all I can think about is them in a wheelbarrow with me pushing. I'm running. There's a lot of rocks in the road, and I have to work real hard to keep the wheelbarrow upright, and to not trip. I'm supposed to get them to the hospital because there's sores opening up all over their body, but I'm thinking it just *has* to be too late. I mean, the sores are filled with pus already. So much pus. It keeps splashing in my eye.

Sometimes when I get real angry, it feels like the cells in my brain are popping and I get very hot on the inside. This causes me to take a step out of the anger for a quick second. I become concerned that this is what it feels like to spontaneously combust. Have you seen those pictures before? It's usually a charred chair, next to it a blackened stump. I will look just like that.

Sometimes when I get in the shower I close my eyes and it seems like I'm no longer actually in the shower. I'm in an alley, and there's a bunch of homeless men pissing in my hair.

Sometimes when I think about what it would be like to be pregnant, I imagine that instead of a baby growing inside me it is a very large worm but with teeth and it is chewing out my uterus. Nine months in, I go to give birth and all that comes out is the worm and its teeth and a lot of blood. The doctors still want me to nurse the worm baby, though. They cradle it and put it in a diaper and give it to me to hold and I am trying to say "No no no" but I am so weak from the birth that all I can do is whine a little. They fold my arms so I am forced to hold it and they latch it onto my breast, which it bites off quickly, and then it's so close to what it was seeking the whole time, which is my heart.

But the funny thing is that whenever I think of you, nothing like this appears. When I think of you, I am helpless and small in your arms and you are stroking my hair. I am helpless and small but I feel very safe; with you I enjoy feeling helpless and small. There is a big big moon and stars dotting maps of smiling lions in the sky and you are singing. The melody causes us to drift up and float, higher and higher, and the stars swallow us, swallowing us in a way that will enable us to always be together, to never bleed or rot, or feel anger or pain, or hurt.

FLAME WAR

Everyone is talking about witch hunts
like they're a bad thing
but I think
it could be fun.
If they had some
maybe I could finally know
how other people looked at me.
Like if they thought I was scary.
Because if it were my choice
I would totally burn myself.
Getting tied up on a pole seems sexy
and as I burned
I could pretend
I was offering myself
up to God.

SEXY TERRORIST

I want to be a sexy monster
unstoppable and
stomping on everything
destroying until it has
all been crumbled
to rubble and powder bones
with nothing to hear but my
howl

I want to be a sexy terrorist
bombs strapped below my
sexy hips explosions burst
on TV news and when
the cops come I am not
afraid to die because
I believe
in things

I want to be a sexy murderer
the scary person breathing
on your phone the one who
shattered your window
left palm prints on the
bed sheets
and stabbed a knife in your
throat

None of this poem is hyperbole
or inserted in here simply because
the images are evocative
of any particular emotional truth.
I really do want to be a

      sexy monster.

      sexy terrorist.

      sexy murderer.

I want to be terrible, powerful, a
force to be reckoned with, which
means I'm
insane.

SEXY TERRORIST PART II

In 2005 my best friend
had a birthday party themed
"Ass, Titties, and Freedom"
so I went dressed as
a sexy terrorist,
which involved a bikini
fake dynamite and
a clock set to 9:11.
I wrote things on my arms like
HELL YEAH AL QAEDA
and
DOWN WITH THE USA
because I was against "freedom"
and found it the opposite
of sexy.
People looked at me
disapproving;
the strangers at the party
would not talk to
me or share
their drugs.
Even my friends said
"Too soon"
– another concept
I disagree with because
there is no such thing.

It is never
too
soon
for anything.

EVERYBODY ELSE

Everyone's always talking about Taco Tuesday
Two dollar beers
Who cares
The kind of deals I care about
are things like the bank's free suckers
I'm an infant

BRO HYMN

They all like Drake but to me he seems like
a real faggot, but they all say
you're not allowed to use that word anymore
which is retarded, if you ask me
but what do I know

INNER MONOLOGUE

WHO CARES WHO CARES WHO CARES
WHO CARES WHO CARES WHO CARES
WHO CARES WHO CARES WHO CARES
WHO CARES WHO CARES WHO CARES
WHO CARES WHO CARES WHO CARES
WHO CARES WHO CARES WHO CARES
WHO CARES WHO CARES WHO CARES
WHO CARES WHO CARES WHO CARES
WHO CARES WHO CARES WHO CARES
WHO CARES WHO CARES WHO CARES
WHO CARES WHO CARES WHO CARES
WHO CARES WHO CARES WHO CARES
WHO CARES WHO CARES WHO CARES
WHO CARES WHO CARES WHO CARES
WHO CARES WHO CARES WHO CARES
WHO CARES WHO CARES WHO CARES
WHO CARES WHO CARES WHO CARES
WHO CARES WHO CARES WHO CARES
WHO CARES WHO CARES WHO CARES
WHO CARES WHO CARES WHO CARES
WHO CARES WHO CARES WHO CARES
WHO CARES WHO CARES WHO CARES
WHO CARES WHO CARES WHO CARES
WHO CARES WHO CARES WHO CARES
WHO CARES WHO CARES WHO CARES
WHO CARES WHO CARES WHO CARES
WHO CARES WHO CARES WHO CARES

YEAH I DON'T CARE

HOW SHOULD A PERSON BE

I was concerned about
coming across as a
bad person
in these poems
but my husband said
I shouldn't worry,
that I was
a mean person,
and nasty,
and I just needed to
accept that,
because we are all mean
and nasty underneath
our skin
and anyone who denies this
is a liar.

WIN FRIENDS, INFLUENCE PEOPLE

I learned by reading two poetry books
– one from McSweeney's and the other
lauded in *The New Yorker* –
that my poems make too much sense.
I need to make less sense.
Three blind mice.

They also need more sex
so here
you
go:

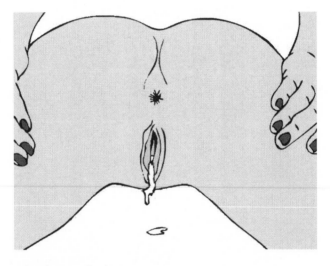

Also I think I might be too pretty.
So it's a good thing I am aging
and gaining weight
because I want the people
to find me
relatable.

SPITE POEM

Remembering the time
when my professor told me
her publicist took advantage
because she was young, attractive, and female.
Except she wasn't that young
or attractive.

BIPOLAR
NATIONAL
ANTHEM

TEEN ANGST

When I was fifteen I tried to kill myself
by swallowing pills and gin.
At the mental hospital they stabbed
my arms
every morning
five am,
with thick needles, not really caring
if they hit the vein first try, just digging.
Pretty quick the crook of both arms
bruised over and scabbed.
The milk in the lunchroom came in bags
meant to be punctured by straws
and tasted like hormones and glue.
I was in there over Fourth of July.
My roommate was a girl named Charlie,
the best cutter I ever met,
scars on her thighs thick as ropes.
She said it went so deep she nearly bled
to death but that she never intended
to die.
Tiny windows in our room scratched-up
shatterproof glass. Through them
we watched the fireworks from Sea World.

CONTEMPORARY GUILT

when i went home
the first time
after going off to get married
my mother begged me: please don't have a baby.

here were her reasons:
1) it would have problems

2) i have problems

3) my husband has problems

4) all the problems would be parts of a real disaster and
   she wouldn't be able to deal so essentially she'd have to
   disown me

predictably, i got mad and
stormed off to what used to be my bedroom.

which is the place where
i tried to
kill myself
four times
half a lifetime before.

in the morning, she apologized
– kind of –
asking if i understood what she meant
that she was speaking
out of love
but also fear.
she told me there were things

she never told me
because she had to pretend to be strong.
i think that was when i was supposed to ask
about the things i never knew
but i failed to.

a few days later, i asked her when she knew
that i'd turn out "okay"—
eighteen, twenty-two, twenty-five?
but she was honest
and said it didn't come until i was
living in new york,
two years sober.
that she used to watch the wine bottles pile up
my skin yellow
teeth darken
and that smell.

i guess that's a long time to be
worried
that your daughter is going
to die.

HANGING FROM THE FAMILY TREE

I bake six pies for
Christmas
Clean the house wrap
The presents but later
I am crying
Pulling hair and breaking
Things
Locked alone
In the bedroom with
Him begging me
To open and asking
What is wrong and
My answer –
Nothing.

My father never speaks
Of his dead mother
Because
She used to beat him
When I asked one
Time what
She
Was like he described a
Woman
Who acted just
Like
Me.

HELP DESK

somet
imes
it's ha
rd to k
now if
you're
still al
ive so
here i
s a su
refire
way to
tell:

MEDICAL PROBLEMS

If one cattle
gets sick
you must kill
the whole lot,
corral them in
a pen and
shoot off
their heads.
It helps
if you play
red queen.

There is only
one way
to prepare my
pneumonic device:
breathing
fresh air until
the letters forget
what it is
they help to
remember
and/or make
sick.

If you blow
into
the stick
the man
inside
the pipe
will smile.

If you do it
hard enough
something else
will happen.
That part is a
surprise.
That part is up
to you.

An allergy test means
pokes
– needles and swabs –
perhaps something else.
When they stick it
inside
your vagina
don't forget
to register
the presence
of blood.

The staples in
my arm
were put there
by a country
doctor he had
to do some numbing
first it came inside me
never forgetting the
smoke clouds
never forgetting
the hour
of my
birth.

I wanted a
loophole
so I made one
out of rope
inside it I put
my head
in the end my
feet dangled the
bracelet
explaining my
condition
dangled off my
toes I dangled
off
the earth.

WHO SAYS THAT FAST FOOD CAN'T BRING A SPIRITUAL AWAKENING

the feeling would be
of summer with the window
open
while on a mild-to-moderate
dose of synthetic opiates
and having forgotten temporarily
that one existed
after vomiting
a small order of
onion rings and
chicken fries
from burger king

LIFE IS A JOKE SOMETIMES

I went to a new psychiatrist
today. I had to drive an hour
to get there
because the ones
in this town just want
to get you high.
I had to tell her my story.
The whole thing.
The suicide attempts, the drugs,
the hospitalizations,
the relationship I had
as a teen where he left bruises.
At the end, she told me
I was a poster child,
the ideal result of someone
with a story like mine.
Which is funny because
I've never felt like
the poster child
for anything.
Yep. That's me.
The poster child
for mental health.

TOP 10 GREATEST FEELS

10.
Going to work, which means putting
on the same black skirt and
blouse as yesterday, taking your
apron from your locker,
smoking a quick cigarette,
and resigning to the fact that
today is the same as yesterday
and neither likes you
very much.

9.
Sitting on a hospital bed
with the lights out because
you insisted and
the orderlies are afraid
which seems... bad...
because they've probably
seen a little of everything,
so it turns out you're a
unique snowflake
after all.

8.
One of the things about
death
is it just gives you another
justifiable reason
to be angry.

7.
There's at least
five people out there
who genuinely hate you
and there's no way to
apologize because
none want to speak to you,
so maybe that's not that different
from actually having been
absolved.

6.
Four am, nightlight projecting
his shadows on the walls
and the pills have kicked in
but you're still there,
still awake,
feeling the invisible bugs
crawl around on
your skin
which, in some ways,
is a kind of
conjure.

5.
Drowning in a pool of water
that may or may not
actually be there
while listening to 1983's
number one hit record
and not really giving
a shit
either way.

4.
Accepting at age thirty
that you've never been in any
position to take care of
yourself,
that a rose garden
is more
self-sufficient,
so why not let
someone truly love you.

3.
Realizing it's impossible
to differentiate the mistakes
you've made from those
that were merely stupid
decisions,
but fuck wisdom
anyway.

2.
Getting to the point where
hearing that one song
no longer makes you feel
ashamed, and the scent
of coconut rum no longer
reminds you of your own
shoddy attempt
at death.

1.
What's the point of wondering
what the future holds
when the past makes absolutely
zero sense at all.

NATURE POEMS
ARE BORING

ON THE CONSTRUCTION SITE
BEHIND MY HOUSE

If you want to make a road
you have to cut down some trees,
light some bushes on fire.
Watch the rabbits run away,
fleeing their homes and tiny babies.
Yep, that's why it's good
to be human.

FUR TRADE

I had a dream the other night where I was a bear.
I had caught myself after
spending several afternoons tracking my scent.
I took a knife and dragged the tip across my bear throat
bleeding a curtain of rich bear blood before
turning the knife to split myself down,
the gentle peeling of my bear belly.
My insides spilled out
in the prettiest shades of purple and red.
I pulled them out slowly,
heavy like jewels in my bear hands.
I gave them to you.
I presented them to you as a necklace.
You put it on and it
looked so lovely against your eyes.

ANIMALS IN WINTER

My first winter somewhere cold and
animals staying alive seems impossible
because I thought "hibernation" meant
holing up somewhere and going to sleep
for a long while
which, as a human, is just called
giving up.

Turns out it means hearts beating
half as fast and
body temperatures
falling near freezing.
Cold veins, a slow heart—
a means to survive.

THE SCENIC ROUTE

We were going the back way to the post office
driving through the alley
behind Lowes and the Walmart where
the workers smoked cigarettes in secret.
It had just rained
and everything glistened.

There was this big field, fenced in but
With nothing in it to protect
except for hundreds of crows.
I asked why the birds were there
and he said that's just what crows do:
hang out together in fields.

But then I looked a little closer
and there was this dead dog,
I think the one we'd seen wild
behind our house, the one I wanted
to trap so it didn't freeze that winter.
Anyway, it was dead.

Stomach bloated, legs stiff out,
pointy in rigor mortis.
The crows were eating at it,
making a lot of noise and cackling.
That's the real reason why they were there.
Dog party.

HAIKU FOR HORSE HATERS #1 – FOUR-FINGER DISCOUNT

every time i look
at your teeth i think about
bloody stump fingers

HAIKU FOR HORSE HATERS #2 – THE JOKE'S ON YOU

if i break my leg
i just go to the doctor.
you do it, you're dead.

HAIKU FOR HORSE HATERS #3 – EXOTIC PETS

down in tijuana
people paint you black and white
and call you zebra

HAIKU FOR HORSE HATERS #4 – DUMB BITCH

shoved nails in your foot
burnt my name onto your rump
now you know you're loved

HAIKU FOR HORSE HATERS #5 – REAL TALK

this isn't a joke
i really do hate horses
they should all just die

HOW TO TALK TO GHOSTS

1. Turn off the light.

2. Make sure your eyes are

W   I   D   E

O   P   E   N

3. Start to cry.

4. When you ask yourself why you are crying, remember there is

n
o

r
e
a
s
o
n

5. When there is nothing left

6. Open your

M

O

U

T

H

and begin

7. To speak

8. But please remember to say

        nothing

of substance

              because
              one
              must not
              frighten

the

ghosts

RELOCATION

FLIGHT 6256

The baby
is screaming
like I want to
scream
and the man's bald spot
looks so soft
I want to pet it
and I don't see
any time
in between.

There is an amusement park
on the ground with
rollercoasters
like shoestrings
and the hills still
hold green leaves but
when we took off
what lay beneath
was a snowstorm
and coal mills
and a graveyard.
One hour
can change nothing
and so much.

SAGA OF A TREADMILL

Today
at the gym
I saw a man
yell at another man
who was one of my husband's
former students.

The student apologized for
whatever he'd done
which caused
the angry man
to grow angrier, wanting him
removed from the gym
because I guess that's what
he thought should happen
when one man
speaks to another
while sweating.

I went home and told my husband.
He said the student was
mentally retarded, the
kindest person you ever met,
not a mean bone in him
– the kind of thing you say
about another person
when trying to paint them
as blameless.

His mother was a drug addict
who later OD'd.
He didn't like to speak of her.

He was certain she was burning
in hell.

MAKE A FIST

I always liked the way
it felt
when the needle
slipped in
as they took my blood
except one time
they dug too deep and
it spilled
all over
the linoleum.

My mother
never speaks
about her family;
if you ask,
she just brings
it right back
to me.

When you fly over
the west,
the earth
has cracks you'd
never be able
to see out of
from the ground.

CHEMISTRY LAB

Behind my house is a fence
the other side is bottles
some containing nothing
some containing meth.
Inside plastic the crystals
glow brighter
than what you gave me
including my own bound
wrists.
A science fact:
Blood is redder
after midnight.
Another:
Forgetting has
no atomic weight,
memories
heavier than just about
anything
but the funny thing is
the absence of a
nucleus.

THIS POEM WAS MADE POSSIBLE BY MONEY AND A FEW MOVEMENTS OF MY HAND (WHICH MAKES IT NO DIFFERENT THAN ANY OTHER POEM)

```
Foxcroft Shell, 619
1000 Foxcroft Avenue
Martinsburg, WV  25401


          05/24/2015 3:32:08 PM
   Register: 1 Trans #: 5012 Op ID: 1921
          Your cashier: Alice

        *** PREPAID RECEIPT ***

REGULAR CA    PUMP# 2           $25.00  99
SIMPLY LEMONADE W/               $1.99 102
DIET MT DEW                      $1.79 101
MARS MILKY WAY S C               $1.29 102
HRSHY TAKE 5                     $1.29 102
S JIM GIANT CRACKD               $1.69 102
                            ----------
Subtotal =                      $33.05
                    Tax  =       $0.11
                            ----------
Total =                         $33.16

            Change Due  =  $-66.86

Cash                           $100.02


    NEVER PAY FULL PRICE FOR GAS AGAIN!
    Join the Shell Fuel Rewards Network
     for free and save money on gas when
   you purcahse specially marked products.

      ROCs Customer Service Hotline
          1 (304) 262-5088
```

GOOD NEWS: GENTRIFICATION IS POSSIBLE EVERYWHERE

In winter I wanted
Adventure so we
Drove through the
Fog to the Old Stone House,
A building that was
Old and dilapidated,
Two qualities he
Thought I'd
Enjoy.
The house was
Registered, an
Official historic site,
Marked with a
Sign at the fork
Off the interstate.
When we arrived
It no longer looked
How he'd remembered it,
Now remodeled, its walls
A sunny stucco,
Bright Christmas lights
Hanging off the
Eaves. In the driveway
Was a Suburu, outfitted
With mountain bikes
And kayaks; you could
Tell the residents were
True people of nature,
Evolved and
Spiritual; you
Could see it in the
Bumper sticker that
Read "Namaste."

DOUBLE EXPLOITATION

Chris's girlfriend came over
and told us about her brother
who wrote short stories,
an Iowa grad.

How he exploited
all the things
that had made her
childhood
hers.

The worst was a man named
Kenny who was
mentally disabled
and gay.

Her first boyfriend
gave him a
blow job
so he would buy beer
for the party
where they first hooked up.

In college she
went over to Kenny's house
after his birthday; he'd been out to a
gay bar
the night before –
had bought condoms
expected romance, but left
lonely
and dejected.

He had a pen knife
because he liked to cut
himself
when things were bad,
so she took it away
and calmed him down
but when she left,
she gave it back, so
the cutting reverted to
his decision.

Kenny is probably
dead now
but his exploitation
lives on.
Long live the
exploitation
of marginalized
people.

THE NAME OF THIS POEM IS A PICTURE

We walk around your parents' house and you are
telling me how when you were in high school
you used to
pretend you were on English moors
but all I can see is
West Virginia.

The sky is only light enough
to catch the edge of trees
how they bleed and feather
into mountains.
There are bats.

We walk to the property line
and look at the forest
and it is so dark at first
there is nothing to see
but if you wait
sky pokes in through branches.
Something old waits
trying to push us out
trying to pull us in
it wraps around our wrists and
things are flickering. It is making me feel
a little restless.

And then a dark thing
creeping
screeches at us. It's sudden.
I forget my breath
until I notice its shape
which is the same as me and you.

It is familiar and so
I feel okay again.
We wave at ourselves.
We are calling to ourselves.

TRUE ROMANCE

LONG DISTANCE LOVE POEM

Three things drew me to you
and none of them can I name right now,
but that doesn't mean they don't exist.

Sometimes I sleep until the afternoon
and still won't get out of bed.
My purpose would be to listen
to you breathe, if you were here,
except you're not and so I have none,
but that doesn't mean I'm not conscious of your breaths.

I read the Wikipedia article for nicotine last night.
In small doses, it is a stimulant,
at larger ones, a sedative.
Which is similar to the effect your hand has when it's on my
thigh.

ASTRAL PROJECT MY PUSSY

Sometimes when I am
having sex with
you I like
to pretend that I am no
longer inhabiting my
body.

Not because I don't
enjoy it but
because it seems
counterintuitive
for what we
are trying
to accomplish.

There is no joy
in arms no
intimacy
in knees no
transcendence
in toes
so let us
dissolve
their existence.

BUT DO YOU LOVE ME

How many cocktail dresses would you like me to shred
before you snip off my toes to make the slipper fit?

How many licks of sunshine does it take to grow cancer on
my face,
and if you were a doctor, would you cut it out yourself,
or would you get a doctor friend to do it for you?
Would you eat it if you knew it would make me feel
beautiful?

If I had a rope for a tongue, would you swing from it
and leap from me into the water,
or would you rather wrap it around your neck, kick the chair,
and dangle
until you were blue
      and cold
      and dead?
Because either is fine by me.
I don't care.
I just want you to be the one who makes the decisions.

IS THIS WHAT YOU WANTED

If you promise to
love me, I will
promise to
never act like
myself for
you.

FAIRY TALE BEFORE BEDTIME

It took me a while to realize
that rain drops were
falling on my
head.
Remember the corpse of
the kitten you buried
in the forest
right after
we met.
I would like to buy its
bones back
encircle them into a
halo
wear it on top of
my head.
Put on bleeding shoes
with silver soles
while holding you
Pop a bottle of
champagne feed you
cake and call it
a wedding.

THAT WAS THEN, THIS IS NOW

The first time we were together on purpose
we walked through the streets of Philadelphia in the rain.
Neither of us lived there and I made a Tom Hanks joke.
You wanted to get a cab but I wouldn't let you,
my reasoning being that a cab costs money
and walking is free. You still drank then,
and your hands were shaking so
we stopped to buy you beer and I waited for you
outside the store, a few feet from a homeless man,
who almost said something to me but thought better of it
when he saw the look in my eye,
something in it more unhinged
than him.
We went back to the hotel and ordered pizza
we never ate because
neither of us were healthy enough to have appetites.
I wouldn't let you touch me but
that would change in a couple months,
because by then I no longer smelled
the scent of death in your footsteps.

HANDLE WITH CARE

When you tie me up
please be sure to break
my body as I
am no longer
any good
at breaking it
myself.

Please feel free
to remove
my skin,
peel me like
a vegetable,
make me smaller,
into a desirable
shape and eat
me because
I want to be
bite-sized.

When we go to bed
do not forget
to set fire to
my hair;
this is the only hope
I have for
being smarter
in the morning.

If you feel the
need to forget
me in the car on a

hot day, there is
no need to lower
the window my blood
needs a good boiling
anyway.

FIGHT POEM #1 – AMPLE APOLOGY

Sorry for kicking you in the stomach.
I didn't know you were in there
until you were
balled up in the corner of the bathroom
and screaming.
I swear it won't happen again.

FIGHT POEM #2 – BEDTIME STORY

The Dateline last night was about a preacher
who killed
each of his wives.
I can't see a bit of that inside you.
Although there was that time I woke up from bad dreams
begging for a promise
that you wouldn't murder me.
That was weird.
Maybe I meant to say it to myself
about myself.
That seems a lot more likely.

FIGHT POEM #3 – NO COFFEEMAKER

We got into it because
he wouldn't get the coffee
and he knows how I am
in the mornings

from the Seroquel.

A point well understood
until his doctor put him
on the same medicine.
But he doesn't need a bra
for the hotel lobby.

His refusal seemed absurd, like
inconveniencing me on purpose,
so I picked up his backpack and
removed the contents, dropping
each item individually on the floor.

At the time
it felt biblical
– an eye for an eye –
but looking back, I admit
it was a dick maneuver.

FIGHT POEM #4 – WHERE'S THAT MIRROR

He kept on asking me
if I was OK, implying his awareness
of my emotional states
was greater than my own.
And maybe it is.
Maybe I still
do not know myself.

FIGHT POEM #5 – BROKEN PROMISE

I told my husband it
was time for working,
not kissing.
He said if I
didn't kiss him
he would jump
out the window.
I didn't kiss him but
he didn't
jump.

FIGHT POEM #6 – DRAMATIC RECREATION

Most of our arguments are over
something stupid and
this one was
no exception.
In this one, I was
the bad guy, the
one who had
a temper tantrum for
no reason.

Later, that night
before bed, I had you
recreate my actions
from earlier, which involved
foot stamping, spinning in
circles, hands over ears,
and exaggerated cries.
Damn.
I looked cool.

TRUE ROMANCE

I.

I'll let you fuck me
if you make it quick.
Like mechanized.
Like we both come
and that's it.
No funny business
in between.

II.

Now that irony
has been milked to death,
what is left?
You wearing a fake beard
while riding me?
I'd like to bear
your weight, carry you
until I collapse,
carry you
until I die.

III.

It's funny that the
first time I
kissed you,
you were a fat
sad drunk,
suicidal with your skin

sweaty and red.
I must have been
real desperate
or in love.

IV.

The one time
during sex when
you told me
you wanted a
Subway sandwich
without realizing
how it sounded.

V.

When I went back
to California you
caught the flu and shit
all over the bathroom
and in the tub.
I made you bleach everything
before I would go in there
but a couple days later
I was taking a bath
and I saw
what might have been
a speck of shit
on the side of the tub.
I didn't wipe
it away.
Instead I bathed
in it.
I'm still bathing in it.

I will always be bathing
in your feces.

VI.

Unseasonably hot
the day
of our wedding,
so you padded your suit
with paper towels in hopes
of soaking up
the sweat.
It didn't work.
Dancing with you
made my cheek wet.

VII.

I held up my hair
off my neck and asked
you to describe to me
the pimple that
was growing there.
It is huge and nasty,
bright red, you said.
It looks like a boil.
It looks like something
died there.
But then you kissed it.

VIII.

We showed up early
to the birthday dinner
so I told you to park next

to the dumpster
and made you jerk off
in front of me to kill
time.
I giggled at you,
the faces you made,
but yeah, I was a little
aroused.

IX.

The one time I picked
my nose
and you ate
my booger.
The time I sent you
fingernail clippings
in the mail.
When we cut our palms
with straight razors
and blended together
our blood.
I am inside you.
You have become
my home.

X.

There are ten sections
in this poem
because you are
obsessed with the
number ten.
Whoever said
I wasn't a
romantic.

```
        10                  10 10 10 10
   10 10 10             10 10 10 10 10 10
      10 10              10 10          10 10
      10 10              10 10          10 10
      10 10              10 10             10 10
      10 10              10 10             10 10
      10 10              10 10             10 10
      10 10              10 10          10 10
      10 10               10 10          10 10
      10 10              10 10 10 10 10 10
10 10 10 10               10 10 10 10
```

FEAR AND
SELF-LOATHING
IN VARIOUS STATES

HOT NEW DIET TIP

This man is saying that the reason
we weigh less in the morning
is because of our breaths
– that they weigh something –
atoms of carbon and water vapor.
But what about the weight of thoughts.
In the mornings, I have so few.
Maybe, in time, I can grow stupider,
grow thinner,
weigh less.

SCIENCE EXPERIMENT

has anyone ever
tried bloodletting
as a remedy
for psychological
maladies

if you need a
volunteer i wouldn't
mind giving it
a go

i mean, i've got
a knife
in my hand
already
so it wouldn't be
that big of a
deal

ALL I'M ASKING FOR IS PERFECTION

Everything on you is oily, and everything on you smells bad. The acne is spreading. There is always something that needs covering up. There are always pimples to pop, impurities to expel, and there is only so much the creams can do. The doctor writes you a prescription and forbids you from sunlight. The directions on the tube say APPLY TO AFFECTED AREA but it seems impractical to cover your entire body. Maybe it would be better to eat it. That way you could fix things from the inside.

In the shower, you use the razors that advertise the closest shave. You use special shaving cream that promises the same thing. Afterward you still feel the hairs under your skin so you shave over and over and it is still not completely smooth so you do it harder. You know the hair will begin to grow back immediately anyway. You know it will be spiky again in the morning. Once you're out of the shower, your legs are red and raw and some of the follicles are bleeding. You rub lotion into them and it feels like you're standing in flames.

Long nails are preferable and so you grow yours out. You apply many different ointments to help them along. They're always manicured. The long nails and the polish make your long fingers look even longer. People comment in a way that sounds complimentary but you're not sure; most use words like "graceful" but someone else says "spindly." You discover that it is hard to keep nails this long clean. Everything wants to hide under them: crumbs of food, cosmetics, snot. In traffic, you get into the habit of using one fingernail to clean out another, and what you remove is always pasty and and grey. At work you watch them fly over the keyboard. They look venomous and sharp, like spiders. In the morning, there are scratches on your cheek, three of them, and it is like the devil has been inside your room.

When you were little, you and your father drove out to the high desert. There were wide expanses filled with white pointy windmills, incomprehensibly tall and spinning. Your father said the windmills were good, that this was the cleanest way for us to get power, and he was a person who knew about such things so you knew it was true. The windmills didn't look like good things, though. The blades looked sharp and in them you saw three versions of yourself, each stabbed with a windmill blade in the back, spinning around, too high for anyone to reach, too high to be saved.

THERE'S BLOOD ON MY SHOULDER

Dear Liza, dear Liza.
So fix the hole.

Q. With what shall I fix it?
A. Someone else's hole.

SATURDAY MORNING

In a cheap hotel my friend
prepared a needle
on the bed
sitting next to me.
When he shot himself his
eyes rolled back before
closing and his body
surged in a way not dissimilar
to electrocution.
I thought for a moment he had
died,
a problem because I would not know
what to do
with his body

but he did not die.

We flipped on the TV and
it was Sesame Street.
The sun was slipping through the
blinds
and I felt surprised by both this and
that the characters and lessons
on the TV
were no different
than when I was
as a child.

BAPTISM

In the bath I watch
my body float and
I am
unable to distinguish
stretch marks from
razor scars.
My right breast is
definitely bigger
and uglier
than the left
though.
My feelings for the
fat
on my stomach
waver;
the lumps are
a good meter for the
type of man you've
snared:
if he compliments,
or ignores.
I married the
kind of man
who kisses it
which should make
me feel beloved
but instead I just
feel obeast,
a fat fuck.

AN INSTANCE OF REVERSE PSYCHOLOGY

J-Woww's fiancé calls their new daughter "Angel Baby" and
means it,
When she goes to get vaccinated he cannot stand to see her
cry
Because angel babies come down from heaven.

When I was a teenager my mother took to calling me angel
child
My father and even her best friend got in on the act
Years later she told me she thought if she
Said it enough
That maybe I would act like it
Instead of poco diablito, which is what they
Jokingly
Called me when I was a kid
When I obeyed and got excellent grades.

WHAT MOTHER USED TO SAY

My hands are cold and my
heart is an
asshole

IT'S WHAT'S ON THE INSIDE THAT COUNTS

I would like it if I didn't see my acne
as a manifestation of my inner self
but this is difficult when my thoughts resemble swine
and there is nothing in my heart worth admiration.

I have picked my face until I bled
and cried later over the scabs,
frustrated at my inability to remove myself
from myself.

He says my preoccupation is one of pretty people,
someone with the luxury to focus on spots,
but I see it as something fitting to plague
a woman incapable of unshackling
her adolescence.

TRUE STORY

The most honest act I can do
is pop a pimple and watch
the pus squirt onto the
mirror.
Everything else is
dishonest,
deceitful,
a cover-up.

ANXIETY ATTACKS

JANUARY 3, 1999: PORTLAND, OR

I pocketed a box of Coricidin at the drugstore the night before I was set to go back. In the morning I swallow half the box with a glass of orange juice and finish packing my suitcase. Soon it is time to go. My scalp is tingling a little bit but mostly I don't feel anything yet. My mom cries some when she drops me off, but it doesn't really bother me that I have to go, and I wonder briefly if this makes me a bad person.

The plane is about to board and now I feel a little dizzy but that's about it. Maybe you're supposed to take the whole box, I think. I swallow the rest of the pills with warm water from the drinking fountain and get on the plane.

When it comes time to transfer flights in Portland, I stand up and it is like astronaut boots on my feet. I walk through the tunnel from the plane into the airport in what at least feels like a straight line. A cigarette seems like the kind of thing that will make me alright but it's not like I'm exactly thinking clearly. I am rushing past the security check point and maybe I hit someone with my backpack because there's this guy and he's glaring at me. He says something or maybe he yells it but I can't quite make out his words. I get outside and light a cigarette. I smoke so fast the end turns long and skinny like a pencil. I focus everything I have onto that red tip and for the five minutes it lasts I feel OK.

I make it back through security and to my gate without too much trouble. The plane is delayed. I am sitting there listening to my headphones, telling myself everything is fine, I will get on the plane soon, but suddenly my head is so thick I can't breathe. Maybe I am ODing. When my fingers go numb I make myself get up and go into the bathroom. I splash water on my face. I don't dry it off. I lock myself in the handicapped stall, sitting on the toilet, head between my knees, trying to catch my breath. When everything has mostly stopped, I notice that the ends of my hair are wet from something, wet from something that is on the floor of the bathroom. It might be piss.

When I leave the bathroom, my pulse is still jumpy but I'm mostly OK. The plane has all boarded. I make it on just in time. When Wade, the afternoon counselor, picks me up in the white van he doesn't seem to notice anything, and my drug test comes back clean, but I feel dizzy and doomed for two more days.

JULY 23, 2001: SAN DIEGO, CA

I took acid a week ago and I probably shouldn't have. Ever since, and things have been sliding around. Shadows vibrate and phones ring and there's no shadows or phones actually there.

I am smoking cigarettes at the tables at the strip mall where we all hang out. Some people are playing cards. I am not playing cards. I am sitting there, doing nothing, just smoking. People are saying things, joking, talking with each other. I have nothing to say. I try to come up with something but everything in my brain is just noise.

My breaths get short and I know I have to get out of there, tripping over the heavy metal chair as I stand up. I walk quickly until I am out of sight, and then I run. I go behind the movie theater, where there is a stucco wall fencing in the theater's emergency exits. I lay down on the cement. It is cold. I take deep breaths and look at the sky. The sky is warm. I have a Sharpie in my pocketbook and I pull it out. I am lying on the cement. I write on it: CEMENT. My head is next to the stairs. I write on them: STAIRS. My legs are next to a wall. I write on it: WALL. I know where I am in relation to other things. I feel them solid under the tip of the pen.

For the next few weeks, when I feel like things are crowding in, I take out my Sharpie and label what's around me. Soon everything at the strip mall has my handwriting on it.

PLANTER
SIDEWALK
CURB
CHAIR

TABLE
ASHTRAY
BATHROOM

The other kids look at me funny when I do this. They already think I am weird and this is just a reinforcing act, but I don't seem to have much of a choice. Maybe they think I'm the charming kind of weird. If that doesn't work—well, at least I have a pretty face.

MARCH 9, 2006: ENCINITAS, CA

He told me he would stop giving me pills when my eyes started watering when I woke up. He said this was a sure sign of addiction. My eyes have been watering for a month at least but he hasn't noticed, or if he has he hasn't said anything yet.

He lives in the garage at his mother's house. It is a separate building and soundproofed, so even though it's at his mother's house there is more privacy than at my apartment, so most nights we sleep here. It is always dark when we wake up because there are no windows, and I look at this as something positive.

We have to go into his mother's house to get coffee. Because of this, I have to wait for him to get up. Last night I couldn't sleep and I'm especially tired. He takes a long time to get fully awake. He, like me, always does it slow. He's the kind of person who you shouldn't talk to in the mornings until he's good and ready. I forget this today, and soon we are arguing.

"Look at your eyes!" he screams at me. "Watering like a fucking junky."

I don't think about the fact that if I am a junky, then he is *really* a junky. I don't think anything logical like that. Instead, something in me snaps, and I am throwing things, CD cases and the wine bottles from the night before, and the wine bottles from the night before that, and they are all exploding against the wall, pop pop pop. He grabs my shoulder to get me to stop. He doesn't mean to be rough, but his fingers are rough anyway because of how I am moving. His fingers feel the way they used to with the boyfriend who was two boyfriends before him, the one I had to get a restraining order against, and the strength behind the fingertips splinters something and suddenly I am on my back nearly choking, and everything is evil, and I am dying, and I can't feel my legs or my arms.

"Breathe," he says, and strokes my hair. I want to swat him away but I can't. He puts a Xanax between my fingertips and I take it to my mouth and chew it up and soon everything slows down enough for me to see straight again.

APRIL 24, 2012: BROOKLYN, NY

I don't really know how it happens but we are fighting in our bedroom and the mirror from the wall ended up on our bed somehow? And then it broke and shards and pieces got all over the sheets, and we were wrestling in it, wrestling for the bracelet she had given him but also for control and neither one of us could find any. It ends with him on top of me because he is bigger and stronger. We are breathing hard, our hearts pounding, and the slivers of glass dig into our skin. His face is in front of mine, his big hands on my shoulders, and I hate it that he has won. So I spit in his face.

Later, I see that me spitting is the demarcating line between what was before and the end of our relationship. But at the time it didn't seem like that big of a deal.

He gets off me, and is going out the door, and I am chasing him, but his lead is too much and I am not wearing shoes, and I have no idea where he went. Probably to one of the bars a few blocks away, but my hair is a mess and I can still feel glass in me and I am too ashamed to be in public and searching for him like a jilted woman. So I go back home.

Except besides not having shoes, I also don't have keys or a cell phone and I can't get back into the apartment. I sit on the stoop and although it's a warm night it is still April and it is cold and my feet are cold and I realize that my life with him is going to end now, that one of us will have to move out, that it will probably be me, that he won't be in my life anymore, that I am alone, that I am ugly, that we just yelled and broke things and wrestled in shattered glass on our bed, that I spat in his face, and my feet are cold, and it is cold, and I am locked out, and the world is spinning, and I am worried I am dying and the edges of things grow dizzy and black.

But then a raccoon is crawling up the fence. There is no wilderness anywhere near us, and I've never seen wildlife around here before, and seeing this raccoon here feels like something meaningful. It is perched at the top, looking at me, deciding if I am a threat, weighing its choices. We regard each other for a while. Then it hops my side of the fence and walks slowly down the street, in the direction of where the person who is now my ex-boyfriend has gone, and I can breathe, and things are terrible and ugly and I am still ashamed but I also know things will be OK without him.

OCTOBER 26, 2014: SOMEWHERE IN OHIO

The night before we did a reading in Indianapolis, and now we are driving back home. I haven't been around people that much lately and we stayed up late and I woke up feeling headachey and dehydrated and anxious, the way I did back when I still drank and was hungover. When we stop at a gas station, I buy a pack of cigarettes to complete the feeling, even though I have supposedly quit.

There is so much roadkill this time of year. Some places on the pavement, it is hard to tell if it is paint that has been spilled or blood.

Somewhere in Indiana and we see this deer walking in some grass on the side of the interstate. Its hindquarters look like they have exploded but it is still upright. Neither of us can tell whether it has been shot or run over.

A few weeks ago, I found a picture of a deer with its stomach slit in a magazine and I cut it out and put it above my desk. Now I feel guilty, guilty for conjuring this animal on the side of the road, this thing that is still alive but suffering, this thing that will almost certainly die soon. Its pain and its blood are because of me.

We get into an argument over CDs. It isn't quite as stupid as it sounds; it has something to do with ex-boyfriends. I end up throwing the CDs and they spill all over the car. He yells at me. I pull the hood of my sweatshirt down as far as it goes, and it covers my eyes and I feel protected from the bright light of the sun and also his anger.

But not really. Soon I am crying. Soon I am crying and I can't stop. I try to think about why I am crying but there is nothing. There is nothing wrong except for everything. I am crying so hard I can't catch my breath. I feel like something has gotten me, grabbed hold of me, is making me crazy, a demon or alien clasping onto my brain. And then I am certain my mom has died, certain something terrible has happened to her, and I am crying because my mom is dead.

Eventually we pass from Ohio back into West Virginia. He pulls over at a gas station. The parking lot looks into a McDonalds. All the lights are on, even though it isn't dark yet, and everything seems to be made out of either plastic or glass. The horizon keeps tilting in the neon light. He tells me everything is OK, and I try to believe him. I stop crying. I check the mirror and there are mascara tears on my face, and I clean myself up.

Eventually I am well enough to go inside. I use the restroom and he buys me a Gatorade. I feel embarrassed because there are a lot of people at the gas station and my eyes are all red.

PREVIOUSLY PUBLISHED:

"Whatever Useless Things," "Handle With Care" – *Prelude*

"David Foster Wallace's Rock Idol Was Axl Rose," "Emotional Truth" – *Dark Fucking Wizard*

"Emotional Truth," "Who Says That Fast Food Can't Bring A Spiritual Awakening," "Bro Hymn," "Saturday Morning," "Spite Poem" – Dostoyevsky Wannabe's *Cassette 86*

"Just the Tip," "Who Says That Fast Food Can't Bring A Spiritual Awakening," "Top 10 Greatest Feels" – *Hobart*

"Recurring Intrusive Thoughts" – *Lazy Fascist Review #1*

"Flame War," "Contemporary Guilt" – *Two Serious Ladies*

"Sexy Terrorist," "Sexy Terrorist Pt. 2," – *The Heavy Contortionists*

"On the Construction Site Behind My House," "Fur Trade," "The Scenic Route" – *Shabby Doll House: The Re-Up*

"This Poem Was Made Possible" – *Forklift, Ohio #31*

"The Name of This Poem is a Picture" – *Ampersand Review*

"Long Distance Love Poem" – *The Bushwick Review #5*

"But Do You Love Me," "All I'm Asking for is Perfection" – *The Quietus*

"That Was Then, This is Now," "Hot New Diet Tip" – *Goblin Reservation*

"Anxiety Attacks" – *Western Beefs of North America*

53767811R00089

Made in the USA
Charleston, SC
19 March 2016